The Bones We Once Belonged To

Powerful word images bring light to living, dying, and life as one moment in time. Judith carries poems into the heart.

Rev. Joan Jiko Halifax
Abbot, Upaya Zen Center

These evocative and beautiful poems dance across the canvas of life and death. Judith helps us wake up to the poignancy of the present moment and what it means to be fully human.

William Ury
International mediator,
Co-Author of *Getting to Yes*

Through skillful craft, Judith Ansara evokes profound images and emotions exploring the depths and conundrums that life presents. What a joy to travel this journey of discovery with her poems as our guide.

Deb and Ed Shapiro
Authors of *The Unexpected Power of Mindfulness & Meditation*

The Bones We Once Belonged To

poems by
Judith Ansara

Earth Shadow Press, Boulder, CO 80304
sacredunion.com   judithansara.com

Copyright © Judith Ansara 2017
All rights reserved.

Printed in the United States of America
First Edition
November 2017

Book Design by Krista Olson and Judith Ansara
Cover Photo: Ilkka Lariola, homeinthewild.com
Author Photo: Dasha Gian dasha-gaian-photography.com

Published by EarthShadow Press, Boulder, CO
judithansara.com
sacredunion.com

dedicated
to women everywhere
your voice is needed in the world

Walkabout

The Visit	5
Borrowed	6
Eclipse	8
Mekong	9
Those Whose Bodies Cannot Be Found	10
Yogyakarta	12
Borobudur Sestina	14
The Storeroom	16
Failure to Deliver	18
These Smiles Are Our Treasures	20
Jet Lag	21

Just This

Waking Up	25
Weeds	26
Serendipity	27
Ahimsa	28
Strange Teacher	30
How Deep	31
Keeping House	32
Cranes Are Yogis Worshiping Stillness	33
Quan Yin in the Garden	34
Small Dance	35
Day in Court	36
Orange Juice	37

Lineage

Stories That Were Never Told	41
Each Morning at Breakfast	42
Namesake	44
Father	45
Color Blind	46
Dojo	47
New England Autumn	48

After His Funeral 49
December 18th 50
Blood, Diseases of 51
Washing the Dead 52
Respite 53
Intake 54
Initiation 55

Arc of Desire

One Persistent Frog 59
The Assignment 60
These Are the Ways We Sleep Together 62
After 63
Midlife Love Sonnet 64
Reflection 65
Day in Bolinas 66
A Particular Fire, The Arc of Our Desire 68
Before We Even Hear the News . . . 70

Liminal

First Thing 75
Li Bai Gets Drunk 76
Erotica 78
Calligraphy 79
Each Night 80
Still Life 82
When God is Calling You 83
Ayahuasca 84
My Teacher Says 86
Ménage à Trois 87
God is Always Making Love to You . 88
Drishti 90
I Hold My Life in the Palm of My Hand 92

Notes 94
Gratitudes 96
Bio 99

this
is an invitation
to the heart of things

Walkabout

The Visit

I am sitting at the kitchen counter
when Aung San Suu Kyi leans over
my shoulder to see what I am writing

I see her reflection in the screen her
cheeks scooped to the bone the lilacs
in the vase next to me brushing her face

our eyes meet across the flickering
space that stitches our world together
invites us to believe we are friends

with those whose lives
are shattered glass mosaics
of unfathomable circumstance

she leans in touches my cheek
her hand warm her breath
a caress of kindness

she whispers in my ear her voice
a rasp of what it used to be
keep writing younger sister

let your voice travel out into the world
it is not enough to leave it hidden
in the cupboards of your comfort

Borrowed

in Vanuatu on a rutted dirt road
our truck almost collides
with an oncoming car

three grass-skirted women
gasp   sound a collective
ahhhhh

wave their reed thin arms
in unison their white teeth
a dazzle of relief

Johanna told me this

strange
how someone else's story
suddenly becomes your own

now my body knows
the synchronized movement
of those beauties

hears their sighs
when disaster misses
by a single instant

and the other story
the one you wouldn't want to see
gets thrown to the threshing floor

how on some narrow curve
or slippery edge   suddenly
an arm reaches

steadies your elbow
takes your story in their own hand
and in that companionable quiet

you are sitting in the shade
watching
with your dark sisters

Eclipse

I
driving north from Bangkok
the moon is slowly disappearing

black smoking mountains
every tree cut and burned

the women walk weary on the road
searching for sticks to cook their rice

II
my friend teaches the villagers
to map their land

around the rock with the jaguar face
upstream sun over left shoulder

past the krathin tree struck by lightening
they know each stone and gully like a lover's face

if they mark it on paper will it be theirs

III
the monks have thousand year sight
without the forests there will be no village

they walk silently at dawn ordaining trees
wrap each tall brother with saffron sash

still
      the question of rice

Mekong

at dawn the boatman glides our dugout
silently upstream as the children trail their fingers
through the murky water call out fish sightings
families of yawning lotus blossoms

they pluck water ferns watch them
go limp and slimy in their hands
place them gently back mesmerized
as they stretch their latticed grace

> *it is an effortless death*
> *to lift a thing from its place*

the jungle has grown back
eating alive the places where the dead have fallen

my children do not hear the gunshots
smell the smoke of the napalmed forest
see the fear blind girl who screams
at the river's edge

Those Whose Bodies Cannot Be Found

vanished bones
whole lifetimes
                                      eradicated
the disappeared
from mountain villages
                                      the neighbors
                                      who would not speak

paralyzed
behind the cupboard door
your sister's scream
silence after gunshot

the children lost to us
ripped from land
that held their stories
                                      stolen generations

young girls in cages
in Mumbai
in Bangkok
eyes with no bodies
                                      bodies with empty eyes

pit at Treblinka
pyre in Tlatelolco
Burundi
Cambodia
Bosnia
Rwanda

too many places
too many people
                                      their names forgotten

we who have lost faith
we who are hopeless
we who close the door
we who try to sleep
we who are well-intentioned
we who wake with outrage
we with our hidden pride
we with our small gestures of compassion

Yogyakarta

the becak driver
peddles us on thin brown legs

our family of five piled in the high
wheeled cart each day he waves as we

tumble from the guesthouse
good morning where you go today

he singles himself out from the dark flock
whose eyes stare at the ground

across the bridges the wide streets
everybody pedals twenty thirty across

wearing western shirts sarongs straw hats
panty hose black briefcase in a casual hand

every day in the hot sun he waits patiently
while we do what tourists do

one day I ask Aatif *how much money do you make*

oh not enough, not enough he says smiling
most goes to the mullah who owns the cart

the next morning we have agreed
to use the money our friends gave us

buy Aatif his own becak
at first he does not understand

then his world breaks open ear to ear

I am not telling you this because I want you
to think us kind but because I want you to see

how his tiny toothless mother
smiled and bowed smiled and bowed

until we were all smiling and bowing
and how his shy wife

gathered their children to her
as I gathered mine

as we pressed our hands
against our hearts

Borobudur Sestina

at Borobudur five hundred stone Buddhas
we circumambulate the pilgrim's path
walking slowly through seven layers of illusion
we should be humbled to our knees
but it is hot the children whine impatient
sculptures of the stages of enlightenment

lost on the young their only enlightenment
shade   coke   a sugar cane   their Buddha
faces strained while those in bas-relief are patient
crawling over obstacles in our paths
wiping sweat beaded behind our knees
dazed - our own small wisdom illusion

waves of heat create miraged illusions
my cherished dreams I hold their enlightened
fragments in the palm of my hand – alabaster knees
folded hard under the serene Buddhas
flinging them they flutter like feathers on the path
forgive me my beloved my impatience

fear renders me impatient
trembling virginal in my illusions
how many thousand times have we walked this path
promising at every death to return enlightened
only you with your dark flamed eyes are my Buddha
only you bring trembling to my knees

below a beggar careens on crippled knees
tourism impaired the guard impatient
a woman coconut-oiled hair her Buddha
belly round with promise the poor harbor no illusions
expect nothing and are thus enlightened
only faith hard work paves their path

we argue over who gets to walk the spiral path
fearful the other's attainment threatens our own knees
raised fighting for first - not very enlightened
wiping the children's faces embarrassed at our impatience
we start up angry then a fading of illusion
tensions melt as we walk the footsteps of the Buddha

when the path ends so ends impatience
we laugh knees sore from effort illusion's
dichotomy enlightened your smiling face the Buddha

The Storeroom
Leros Greece 2015

the women press into the building
urgently repeating *please please*
pushing their children toward me
pointing to their own wet clothes

I clamp my flashlight in my teeth
stoop into the moldy storeroom
rummage in plastic garbage bags
crushed cardboard boxes

I pull out one barely butt covering
mini skirt three low cut tank tops
a gold lamé bathing suit
factory frayed jeans

there are precious few
long sleeved high necked
shirts roomy pants floor length
skirts scarves to cover

worlds away our hands flutter with
helpless compassion we rummage
our closets unable to discern the cut
or fabric of their aching need

please send shoes with sturdy soles
warm sweaters without holes
new pants creased with dignity
loose enough for sorrow

tuck into the pockets
your prayers your own grief
your knowledge that these reaching hands
these frightened children are your own
and that you are nowhere else but here

Failure to Deliver
Leros Greece 2016

we have given them a roof
black metal bunk beds
cast off sheets with flowers
and superheroes to rig up
for privacy three showers
six toilets two with seats and handles
four squats with a green hose
five sinks sometimes there is
hot water sometimes not

we give them two meals a day
rectangular aluminum tubs
white cardboard tops
crimped to cover
pasta with cheese a hunk
of white bread

we are instructed
guard the food
until everyone is seated
until everyone is quiet

we hand out
97 plastic forks
we are told
not to ask their help
some might sneak extra
there is never extra

I break the rules
cannot bear to see them
stripped of dignity
three young men lift
the boxes grateful
for anything to do

silent families shove
food in quickly
no smiles
no dinner time banter
no *how was your day*

we can't give them hope
we have no idea when they will leave
we repeat *I'm sorry I don't know*
over and over until they do not ask
as the slow dusk of depression
flattens them into shadows
of their former selves

we don't give them trust
to organize their own meals
wash their own sheets
teach their children
what they know
what they remember

they are collapsed with waiting
in this liminal space
that will never be their home

These Smiles Are Our Treasures
inspired by a translated facebook post
Matina Kasteveli, Founder, Leros Solidarity Network

perhaps with a little kindness a warm meal a shower a bed an ice cream for the children may they forget for a while the bombs the rape the murders may they forget for a moment all that they have lost all that they can never return to

may they have for a moment safety may they have for a moment welcome may they have for a moment respect may they find a place beyond barbed wire may they find a place beyond hatred may they find a place where they can make a life where their own faith can rise again

Jet
Lag

now home
I can't   quite
            land

my kitchen
its teal walls

baskets on the high ledge
white gleam of formica

drapes still needing to be hung
Robert's familiar touch

I drink strong tea
contemplate quantum physics

the empty space inside my body
larger than
      blood   liver
                    spleen

still wavering   trying to find
the bones I once belonged to

Just This

Waking Up

I resurrect myself from protoplasmic sleep
as the new green of the aspen
knocks at my window

the one that tunneled its roots under
the yard intent to propagate
whatever openness is left

what is this desire to drill
into the heart of the earth
to fill everything with ourselves

each morning new disasters wait
I walk to the lake
crouch feral in the tall grass

the heron lifts her wings
unperturbed by thoughts
of her children's future

Weeds

mock strawberries have been creeping
into the lawn claiming the brown grass
victim of a broken sprinkler the lack of rain

I sit examining the tiny red globes low
snaking vines and enter the time lapse
lens of summer to watch them grow

my phone rings in the kitchen
brushing the dry grass from my pants
I survey overgrown lilacs that no longer bloom

fledgling blackberries struggling to survive
long legged aspen the full bodied maple
where the twelve-point buck hangs out in winter

gone the trampoline the laughter of children
the yard needs mowing weeding pruning
young men with trucks who need the cash

I want to let this wildness grow
find peace with my own invasive species
humans claiming territory better left alone

Serendipity

I sit at the computer wanting to make sense of the world and do something useful to illuminate the growing mess and make amends for all the small transgressions I make every day some are willful acts of sabotage while others cruise the streets like four year olds on speed or catatonics trying to negotiate their total absence sometimes I wonder if there is reason to do anything but look for beauty pleasure wherever I can find it but then sauntering through the chaos a delicate grace chooses me with her kind eyes and for moments which seem to appear and disappear like coins behind the ear I swell with pride we humans with our redoubtable ingenuity churning out small acts of kindness heaving epic tasks on our frail shoulders peeking out from under overwhelm to voice our outrage our burgeoning desire as the world with its idiosyncratic myopia sighs

Ahimsa

as I walk the mowed field's tangle

words   l e a p   like   the   grasshoppers

into

my
mind

luminous
                                          potbellied
                    slothful
                                                        anemone

incessant
drone

I want to use words with precious care

like the Jain of India
white gauze over my mouth
sweeping the path in front of me
against the inadvertent harming
of the smallest thing

Strange Teacher

friends hypothesize the cause
how is your stress level is it allergies not
enough sleep too much computer have you
gotten off gluten off dairy caffeine red wine

everyone wants to fix me
make my migraines stop
this the holy shape of their compassion

I sink into down-filled nest
close eyes in blessed quiet
step onto spaceship breath
weightless gliding

watch as pain I thought was solid
feelings called fear helpless hopeless
shed their names and forms
dissolve into a sparkling incandescence

life brings us gifts we do not want
still we unwrap them
discover walls we can walk through

How Deep

seasoned branches
bear silent witness

the top rail of the fence
the barbecue and picnic table

heaped with snowy domes
behind the picture window

we calculate the inches
appraise the safety of the roads

as if this reckoning could save us
from skidding out of control

Keeping House

September winds have blown
the cottonwoods' white-seeded fluff
onto our deck

each morning new arrivals
outside my kitchen door
I watch their numbers grow

thinking I will wait until it's done
let them gather in ritual surrender
strange grace of the fallen

but today the urge is overwhelming
I take the wide broom pushing hard
against the death that landed here

scraping the corpses into a pile
propelling them down the stairs
into the yard patting them

into an eiderdown around
the hawthorn still full
in its own flowering

Cranes Are Yogis Worshiping Stillness

at the edge of the lake where the cattails
grow deeper every summer

she stands unblinking
waiting for the quick pulse of gills

a nuance of movement
under the dark surface

on another island
our friends are standing

around Charley's bed
silently watching

for his last
feathering breath

Quan Yin in the Garden

lingering white blossoms
surrender to winter's freeze and thaw

the power of water
cracks her stony gown

she sits serene
her face dissolving

Small Dance

stand still

        let your feet grow into the forest floor
          the sidewalk   the linoleum

                        the edge
                            of
                               a
                                   cliff

              notice

breath   bone

              the
                 curve
                  of
                 your
              neck

ache in knee   pain in hip
          space   between   toes

              blood flow

       the tingling that lets you know

              here I am

              just this

Day in Court

you have been charged with multiple
counts of feigned arrogance

undocumented insecurity
impersonating your own résumé

the trial will be a farce
everyone will be in costume

guilty on all counts would be a relief
then you could finally take a nap

you daydream community service
performed in the nude

handing out cans of beans
tubs of mayonnaise

to an endless line
of disembodied arms

when the warehouse is empty
you tie on your mother's flowered apron

step into your exhausted combat boots
close the door behind you

on the rain-slick street a clarinetist
is playing *Free This Woman Blues*

Orange Juice

this morning
before you reconstitute yourself
reconsider
taking yourself so seriously

Lineage

Stories That Were Never Told

faint trail of ancestors
three widows
two paths from the village
the earth we tilled
what we cannot
will not remember

love and its history
put it in writing
still
it will not endure

gnarled trees split gravestones
saffron spiders spread like stars
every moment stark
against your face

in Terezín sand through your fingers
33,430 stories scrawled in haste
15,000 children
the absence of butterflies

three backs bent with
grief
their shape a sacrifice

bury it with me
even this
most haunted
most beautiful day

Each Morning at Breakfast

my grandfather ate his oatmeal with cinnamon
a level teaspoon of brown sugar his black coffee
idle as he folded the Times into vertical thirds
as if he was still riding the subway
from Flatbush to Manhattan

each morning his horn rims
slipped down his nose as he turned
the narrow leaves to the obituaries
his eyebrows almost converging
on the folded fields of his face

after he pushed back from the table
set his blue napkin on the yellow formica
and shuffled out I read them myself
wondering about Dora Feinberg who died
yesterday at seventy-six or Joseph Vitari

who was forty-three and left his loving wife
and three children Carolyn Smyth was a graduate of
Goucher College Al Rosenberg an investment
banker Samatha Daley was only four and her
parents' grief was not mentioned or how

her mother sat every day smoothing
her flowered quilt arranging and rearranging
bears and unicorns I wanted them to say
it was cancer or homicide a tragic accident
or even loneliness

but the paper's silence haunted the air
like my grandfather's private ghosts
who themselves were never mentioned

Namesake

I
Holofernes's army
against the city gates
lost prayers of the people
children suck water from sand
the desert a blazing dance of death

II
robed in indigo stillness
resolution binds her
amber and myrrh
moon gleamed hair
ululations of her women
she has prepared forever
a camouflage of silence

III
an apparition before his tent
pomegranate lips
kohl-rimmed eyes
destiny unfolds
at her jeweled feet
the guard her pawn

> *Shechina*
> *moon mother*
> *dark sister*
> *guide this wine-filled kiss*
> *this trembling hand*

Father

this is my son you will not have

you have cried terror
long enough
strangling
every thing

his sure-footed delight
on ragged cliffs above the sea

I want him to feel   the precipice
I want his bones   to shake
I want him drenched   with awe

we are done closing windows
against the wind

Color Blind

his small hand in mine
we scurry like sandpipers
laugh as waves threaten our feet

the sea glows lavender and scarlet
baffled by my vivid pleasure
he searches his grey horizon

oh Ben I wish you could see
myriad greens of trees
dawn's blessed persimmon kiss

Dojo

he teeters on the precipice
of too much power
I don't need a Mother

his arsenal displayed
fox coyote insult hurler
charmer beggar howler sulker

I long for solitude
the end of argument
oh yes you do

determination claims me
I sit cross-legged on the floor
admiring his pluck

when he is finally spent
my little soldier
falls into waiting arms

New England Autumn

with the slow fading amber
of elder leaves
my father is dying

a final show
of burnished brass
a filigree of veins
crumble
in winter's grasp

mumbling in half sleep
his hand
gestures abruptly
making its closing
arguments

a momentary recognition
with each friend's arrival
then he closes his eyes
attending to the busy work
of decomposing

I wish my mother
would take him home
let him crawl
under his beloved maple
lose his appetite in peace

After His Funeral

fatherless I walk the wooded path
falling sun sharpens
the skeletons of branches

death an abstraction of absence
a formless thing I cannot grasp
or find within myself

a broad oak has shed its yellowed leaves
I pile them into a mound
slip under their familiar comfort

my body composts layers of grief
until I too become
part of the weightless dark

December 18th

I wonder when I erased his birthday

it must have been after my mother died
as if the thread that led me back to him
no longer had a place it could be wound

no gift to be mailed
no voice saying
hi honey I'll get your mother

no one to hear
across the tangled
lines of memory

still

the veins of my hands bulge like his
and the narrow shape of my eyes
so sensitive to light

Blood, Diseases of

too late for transplant
our sister-friend is losing

the corruption of marrow
leukocyte's frenzy

antibodies attack
their own young

death can be delayed
only by drastic measures

chemical cocktail
azerra neosar cytoxan

radioactive isotopes
aimed with precision

on the stainless steel table of grief
our own hearts threaten surrender

we try to follow her pace
not giving up too soon

or holding on too long

Washing the Dead
for Amethyst

we coil around you
a snake of sisters
the ancient knowledge rises

we have been here forever
keening the queen of night

your eldest daughter trails
a touch of jasmine
between your breasts

with rose water and salt tears we wash you
you cool and harden as our fingers
whisper our first farewell

Respite

that last evening
before the hidden cyst
blew your ovary up like a balloon
we feasted on garlic bisque you
savored every velvet spoonful

amber crusted rolls
opened their pliant centers
to the rosemary scented oil

alive with possibilities
you tossed your golden mane
purring through every course

the miracle of three raspberries
on lemon sorbet their dark wombs
surrounded by perfect flesh

Intake

while you carefully roll each starched cuff
I could tell you how my daughter's breath
catches in her larynx   a startled bird
I could show you the flight of fingers on hair on skin
playing the chords of her dark unquiet

while you sit behind your polished desk
make detailed notes on a lined yellow pad
ask each question in the diagnostic manual
looking for the proper codes for her disorder

if you would once look up
I would show you her frozen brilliance
explain how when others praise her gifts
she stands transfixed before the false mirror
cataloguing her imperfections

Initiation

let us dance with our daughters
make amulets of their first blood

like soldiers whose medals marked their valor
we will wear the crimson badges of our own courage

let us bind as sacred their first sacrifice

since the first rites were banned from the forests
since our fertile bodies ceased to bless the fields

since our blood was turned safely to wine
we have been seduced into forgetting

let us guide our daughters' hands to their own bodies
to their own bright flames

Arc of Desire

One Persistent Frog

still pool
echos
its green depths

his voice
a chalice of desire

The Assignment

He said:
write a love poem today

I said:
you are my love poem

        hands
      on my
       body
        your
         lava
          fingers
           b r e a t h e
          me
           ling er ing
           you

            clear the mirror
           my eyes
           my mouth
           your tongue

        slips
        searches

```
            rise
    i              to you
            fall


        o   pen   ing



            fall
        ing
            f
            a
            l
            l
            i
            n
            g
        o   pen   ing

fathomless            dissolve

           until
         i-you-we
        dis  appear
```

These Are the Ways We Sleep Together

in a wide "v" our soles touching
  you snuggled like a child in my arm
    my head on your belly grateful for softness
     with our dog between us
     with our kids between us
       on the far edges of the bed   caverns between us
      you on your back flung wide
        me curled on my side
         you in a hotel surfing channels
          me at home with lots of pillows
           me curved small around your back
            my head on a pillow padding your shoulder
            your arm surfing the curve of my hip
            my leg draped over your crotch
            you nuzzling my neck hand on my breast
           my butt in the concave space of your belly
          our hands entwined heart-shape perimeter
         ripping covers off - my hot flash your adrenaline
        forehead to forehead knees pulled up
       yanking the covers to our own side grumbling
      burrowed under the quilt giggling
    me here   you there
   you snoring   me shoving you over
  restlessly rearranging
 tiredly tolerant
quiet like old friends

After

you　　　　still
in the fibrous sponge
that is my body

morning's
smooth pink rising

now tucked behind
the hills

and I
languorous from touching

remember
in the soft folds of myself
that which remains

Midlife Love Sonnet

we who have lived as trees our roots entwined
young saplings that we were with tender eyes
by love enriched and not by love confined
our leaves and branches canopy our lives

it's hard to see where one begins or ends
we know this over-merging may conspire
our dance composed of bows resists and blends
to douse even the most conflagrant fire

know I'll love you always like no other
but oh my dear I crave a little space
my unique expression to discover
it's time my own dear flames to re-embrace

still our star shines on through droughts and storms
bestowing constancy on changing forms

Reflection

you appear behind me as I floss my teeth
in the mirror time is playing tricks on us

your hand moves down my neck
cups my left breast

without my glasses
we are twenty

sixty   forty   eighty
transparent layers

insubstantial as clouds

Day in Bolinas

you toss seductions like red balloons

if I were to wrap my wrists
they would pull me skyward

our eyes meet in stillness
what do you want I ask

great sex and to be friends
in the thin air of this moment

nothing seems complicated
or preordinate of pain

I will hold the boundary you say
breaking our gaze

we climb the bark-mulched hill
sit staring over green curves of earth

I don't want to leave this grey
and violet dusk but sweat chills me

we run laughing into your nest
eat lentil soup balsamic dressing

on the salad I have washed
at the small sink inches away

as it darkens you unfold your futon
I make us tea with milk pouring its heat

into the almost empty honey bear
for the last drops of sweetness

we read poems to each other
Rumi   Neruda

stumbling over the Spanish
words we will never say

you rub my back through the knobby
yarn of my sweater

a sigh escapes me
even in those few moments

when desire almost tumbles us
even as we catch our breath

even as you drive me on winding roads
up the coast where my husband waits

our hands held easily as sunlight
we toss balloons

that dance on the breeze
catching and holding

just for a moment

catching and letting go

A Particular Fire,
The Arc of Our Desire

acacia lasts for generations
heartwood a covenant
we have not broken

we get up straighten the bed
drift apart the practiced
rhythms of our days

me multitasking making tea
putting away dishes
sipping in solitude

you committed to the health
of your gums waterpik
play boggle scan the news

when the veil of sleep has lifted
we light a candle sit in silence
the underscore of days

a sweet embrace
what are you up to today

behind your office door
you laugh with clients
pound emails like rock piano

I claim the kitchen counter
poems like scattered leaves
a duet of focus and distraction

our passion banked to a slow simmer
we might miss it if we didn't stop
gaze beyond the hearth of the familiar

choose to turn again and again
breathing each other in
as a new flame slowly rises

Before We Even Hear the News

we know we will die

preferably
in a way we can control

no illness or pain
a gentle slide under the covers

we'd live into our nineties
minds still crisp

on good days we'd briefly consider
cleaning the leaves from the gutters

but our children would scold us
take away the keys

we wait for the call that will say if it's cancer

I startle awake dreaming
a dark indentation on his pillow

but his head is still here
its hair not fully grey the lines

I love creep like well-tended vines
from the corners of his eyes

I reach for the warm hand so familiar
I thought it would always belong to me

now I am looking into a future of absence

but it could be me who exits first
my heart bursting — a drunk driver

this thought hurtles me back
as I remember

how perfectly holy this moment is
the only one we can depend on

Liminal

First Thing

before eyes open
give yourself away

let emptiness fill you
with praise
with wonder
each breath
your first
each breath
your last

before tea or teeth
lie on the earth
your prayer rug
the unswept floor

let your heart pour
its avalanche of grief
its fear or celebration
let silence enter you
weave into
your lungs
                    your open mouth

Li Bai Gets Drunk

the poet Li Bai drowned
trying to embrace the moon
after sixty years of exile
he still wanted to know her secret

who could blame him
for wanting what she offered
after fame and degradation
after prison and release

wandering for endless seasons
scratching his poetry
on ancient cliffs leaving
traces of his passing

once in winter snow piled high
Li Bai took refuge in the cradle
of a piñon pine and chanted
the questions that haunted still

there was no answer
in the muffled forest
who would deny him
his final pilgrimage to water

climbing the ship's mast
trying once more to pierce
the veil between this world
and the next

who can blame him
for getting so drunk
he dove deep and finally
caught the light

Erotica

I have a thing for cranes

the way they audaciously rise
slicing the sky

their laddered steel
a pathway to vastness

an improbable exit
from this world

Calligraphy

our teacher asks
how do you know when a painting is done

in the student's hand
brush still full black ink rice paper
jumble of lines

we cluster around
hoping the master
will dispel confusion

hoping we too
can learn to recognize
the one true thing

Each Night

before we fall dark and formless
eyelids flutter
drifting at the edge of sleep
night beckons

eyelids flutter
poised in half-light
night beckons
caught between worlds

poised in half-light
wavering
caught between worlds
until surrender sings us down

wavering
our fragile will dispersed in air
until surrender sings us down
lifts us on invisible wings

our fragile will dispersed in air
drifting at the edge of sleep
lifts us on invisible wings
before we fall dark and formless

as we fall dark and formless
beneath our clouds of sorrows
losing our bearings
compassionate arms embrace

beneath our clouds of sorrows
compassionate arms embrace
guide us into an eyeless void
empty and glittering dark

guide us into an eyeless void
silence waits
empty and glittering dark
bright sea before us

silence waits
body like waves
bright sea before us
phosphorescence shimmers

body like waves
losing our bearings
phosphorescence shimmers
as we fall dark and formless

Still Life

while the oatmeal is cooking
I arrange the lilies that have been standing
in the vase since yesterday

I toast the quinoa dice the onion
for the supper we will bring to David
who has broken his kneecap in two places

time spreads like dawn buttering the sky

we are done rushing towards
our imagined futures spiced
with their mélange of decay

skins of onions random fall
severed stems
sliced with morning light

When God is Calling You

listen

lay down your hat your scarf
your precious life
turn off your phone the hard drive
say *no* to lists and invitations
texts call waiting
googling and *just a minute*
forget the dogs the kids the marketplace
forget the shoulds and have-tos

when God is calling you
lie face down on the earth
unpeel the layers of your self
like ripe fruit
offer your seeds
as supplication
moist flesh as alms

Ayahuasca

she tells me to tilt my head
angling the sharp line of my chin
to the hawk's wing
angling the cloud

sky washed in aubergine
and melon dusk
canyons' black-violet shadows
I lie back on desert sand

she stands at my feet
great dome of belly
mountainous breasts
crest of thigh

her translucent hand
enters me
pulls unfelt sorrows
a glorious storm

waterfalls cascades
magnificent tears
drench the parched
pores of my body

every muscle held
too long every joint
deprived of freedom
every cell bound by fear

yet again she whispers
shows me our covenant
my name inscribed

wraps me in her mantle of golden light

My Teacher Says

add nothing to the instructions
obscure translations
highlighted fantasies
magical incantations

do just what I say
strip yourself of seasons
decorations heirlooms relics
your vast intelligence

pour the pitcher of your mind
into the space around you
what you think happened
or hope or fear will happen

your lists and lamentations
have no place at this table
where emptiness is the only
entrée served

Ménage à Trois

we are walking in the garden
holding hands at dusk

when god shows herself
as a shaft of light

instantly smitten
we shamelessly follow

stumbling through fern and bramble
deep into the woods

until we come to an open glade
where she stands waiting

we fall into her embrace
both of us fools for love

present all you need to do is open the eyes of your heart ever always you to love making always is [curving around left side]

god
is always making love to you

always

      ever present

          all you need to do
is open the eyes of your heart

love
   is always   always

ever present

always

     making love to you

          all you need to do

is open

open

the eyes

   of your heart

life
is always

making love to you

always

ever present

god is always making love to you ever present all you need to do is open the eyes of your heart [curving around continuing] *god is always making love to you always ever present all*

  all you need to do

      is open

           open

            the eyes of your heart

  god is always

  life is always

  love is always

                always

                          making love to you

            all you need to do

      all

you need to do

          is open

              open my friend

            open the eyes

                  of

                  your heart

Drishti

I
While dying:
hold
a steady gaze
love
loss
body
surrenders
offer
your long
breath
out

II
Dedicate:
your
life
leave only
trails
of beauty
of kindness

III
Relinquish:
blame
clean up
your own
mess

IV
Practice:
thoughts
insubstantial
unfindable
you
on belay
the space
between
a slender
filament
of light

I Hold My Life in the Palm of My Hand

unfolding petals
one
by
one

it has taken a lifetime
to even glimpse
the center

                in my hand

                              emptiness

there was no life
after all

only
the folding away

Notes

Walkabout

The Visit
Aung San Suu Kyi is a Nobel Laureate and non-violent activist from Myanmar, who has been an outspoken advocate against the military dictatorship. She endured 15 years of house arrest until succeeding in gaining democratic elections for Myanmar and being elected to Parliament in 2012. She currently serves as head of Myanmar's National League for Democracy. Since the completion of this book Aung San Suu Kyi has been accused of not speaking out against the extreme and brutal persecution of the Rohingya Muslims by the military which still holds almost absolute power.   p. 3

Mekong
Originating in China, the Mekong River flows through much of Southeast Asia and figured strongly in the fighting and narrative of the Vietnam War.   p. 7

Borobudur Sestina
Borobudur is a 9th century Buddhist temple complex in Java, Indonesia. This World Heritage and pilgrimage site is experienced by walking a spiral pathway adorned with narrative bas-relief carvings.   p. 12

Just This

Ahimsa
Ahimsa is a Sanskrit word that conveys the principle of non-harming. Ahimsa is one of foundational precepts of Mahatma Gandhi's movement of non-violent resistance.   p. 26

Quan Yin in the Garden
Quan Yin is the revered Buddhist deity of compassion and mercy, most often depicted in female form.   p. 32

Lineage

Stories That Were Never Told
Terezín (also called Theresienstadt) is an 18th century fortress in the Czech Republic. During World War II the occupying German army turned it into a Gestapo-run ghetto and concentration camp. p. 39

Namesake
The Book of Judith in the Biblica Apocrypha tells the story of Judith using her beauty, intelligence and courage to save her town from the Assyrian army led by Holofernes. Judith gained entrance to his tent, got him drunk and beheaded him with his own sword. p. 42

Liminal

Li Bai Gets Drunk
Based on a popular legend about the famous 8th century Chinese poet, Li Bai. p. 74

Ayahuasca
Ayahuasca is an Amazonian visionary plant mixture that is used in ceremony to provide a doorway into altered states of consciousness. p. 82

Drishti
Drishti, Sanskrit for *focused internal gaze* and a Yogic practice for developing concentration and stable intention. p. 88

Gratitudes

We are all part of a vast interconnected fabric. I honor those known and unknown to me, who have touched my life. During this cycle of my life, a deep bow to Dan Brown and John Churchill for their profound guidance.

To my remarkable community of heart friends, *thank you*.

Leila, Danya and Benjamin — you are lights in my life, my teachers and now my cherished companions. It has been an honor to parent you and a joy to watch you fly.

My profound appreciation and honoring to those who have contributed most directly to the creation of this book.

Lisa Birman, poet and novelist, has been my kickass editor and mentor this past year. Her clear and unstinting feedback taught me to become a better writer. Lisa walked every step of this book with me and her smart and fun companionship helped me thoroughly enjoy the creative process.

Robert Gass, my beloved husband of 48 years whose boundless love, support and commitment is hands down the greatest gift of my life. Whether I was questioning a choice of words, feeling overwhelmed by my disorganized files or figuring out the sequence of poems, he has been my hands on and arms around champion and best friend.

Ginny Jordan, writer, artist and dear friend whose wisdom, poetic skill and artistic perception permeated each suggestion, question and invitation to go further. Her love and commitment to me over a lifetime, and to this book as an expression of that life, is a gift beyond measure.

Krista Olson, who thinks it's normal to go for a hundred mile run in the mountains. She was similarly confident that creating a book design and getting the manuscript laid out and to the printer would also be no big deal. Her skill is formidable and her attitude contagious.

Erin Robinsong, poet and performance artist, was the first person to read my earlier work. Her enthusiastic encouragement gave me exactly what I needed to say a full-hearted *yes* to this book.

Max Regan, poet and teacher, who gave me and countless others the gift of finding their own writer's voice in his wonderful classes. The seeds of some of these poems first sprouted under his tutelage.

Danya River, artist, musician and Somatic Experiencing® practitioner, multi-talented and beloved daughter for recording several poems, designing my website and encouraging me to choose a photo where I actually look my age.

Judith Ansara

Judith had to pass a test to be allowed to start kindergarten before she turned five. *What flies in the air?* asked the teacher. *A kite!* she said jumping up from her chair. The teacher said *No. It's an airplane.* This moment birthed a wariness towards external authority and a life dedicated to helping others learn to trust their own wisdom and direct experience. For over 40 years Judith Ansara has served as a seminar leader, coach and spiritual guide to those committed to fostering a just, conscious, and sustainable world. With her husband, Robert Gass, she also leads retreats for committed couples. A writer, dancer and artist of life, Judith also delights in hanging out with her two beautiful grandsons.

judithansara.com
sacredunion.com